desperate PEOPLE in desperate TIMES

the transition from
PROGRAM TO PRESENCE

PASTOR LONNIE PARTON

Copyright ©2010
ISBN: 978-1-886296-56-5
Printed in the United States of America
All Rights Reserved

No portion of this book may be used without written permission and consent of the author. To contact the author, please refer to the "Author Contact Information" below. Contact the publisher or author for such permissions.

- Unless otherwise noted, all Bible quotations are taken from the New American Standard Bible®, © Copyright 1960, 1962, 1963, 1968, 1971, 1972, 1973, 1975, 1977, 1995 by The Lockman Foundation. Used by permission. www.Lockman.org.

- English Standard Version: Scripture quotations marked "ESV" are taken from *The Holy Bible, English Standard Version*. Copyright © 2000; 2001 by Crossway Bibles, a division of Good News Publishers. Used by permission. All rights reserved.

- King James Version (KJV): Public domain.

Author Contact Information:
Lonnie Parton, Pastor
Victory Fellowship Church
2111 23rd Avenue
PO Box 1843
Council Bluffs, Iowa 51502
1.712.323.3453
lrp@vfministries.com
web *www.vfministries.com*

Publisher Contact Information:
Arrow Publications, Inc.
P O Box 10102
Cedar Rapids, IA 52410
Phone 1.319.395.7833
Toll free: 1.877.363.6889
Fax: 1.319.395.7353
Website: *www.arrowbookstore.com*

Cover Photo by J. Brelsford *www.http://sxc.hu*, ID #603017 titled *"the distant Olgas"*

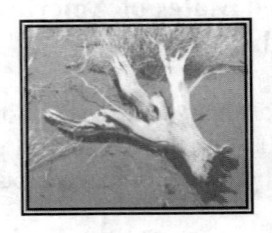

Acknowledgements

To my wife, Carolyn
Thank you for always hearing the Lord
clearly and encouraging me to go for it!
Thanks to the group of Elders who said, "yes" to the Lord in 2004 and for the unforgettable times of prayer, repentance, unity and celebration we have shared.
(Jim Nichols, Scott Maskell and Rick French)

Thanks to our Victory Fellowship Church Family

Thanks to Fusion Ministry, Inc.
(Rhonda Hughey, Dr. Wes Adams and Steve Freeman)
This team has been with us from the beginning to give counsel and encourage us every step of the way in our journey.
You remain our dear friends and co-laborers.

Front Cover Design by Brandon Baker

Dedication

*To our children,
Nathan and his wife, Rebekah,
Emily and her husband, Brandon,
and Benjamin*

SUCH IS THE GENERATION OF THOSE WHO SEEK HIM,
WHO SEEK THE FACE OF THE GOD OF JACOB
Psalm 24:6 (ESV).

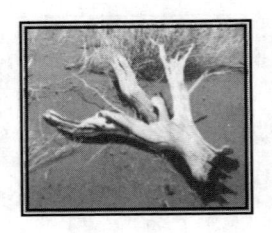

Table of Contents

Introduction
Page 8

Chapter One
It Matters Not What Brings You to Desperation
Page 12
The Promise
Desperate Times in the Church
The Diagnosis
A Different Diagnosis

Chapter Two
Desperation Makes You Do What You Would Not Ordinarily Do
Page 23
Testing Foundations
Personal Confrontations
Wrestling with Presence
Learning to Hear Jesus' Voice

Chapter Three
GOD SPEAKS TO DESPERATE PEOPLE
Page 36
Early Beginnings
Wrestling with the Lord
Public Repentance
Leaning on Jesus

Chapter Four
THE DISTINGUISHING MARKS OF DESPERATE PEOPLE
Page 46
A New Leadership Style
Learning to Wait
Posturing Our Hearts
Jesus is the Reward for Waiting

Chapter Five
DESPERATE LEADERS FOLLOW JESUS
Page 54
The Visitation of Jesus
How Does Jesus Spell Success
More Provoking from God
Turning a Large Ship
A New Evaluation
Finding Partners

Chapter Six
A GENERATION OF DESPERATE PEOPLE
Page 70
A Restored Identity
A Generation Who Prays
Proactive Fasting

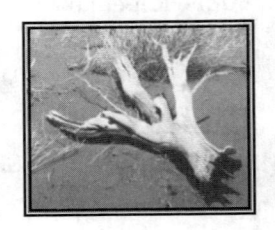

INTRODUCTION

*"And the mirage hath become a pond,
and the thirsty land fountains of waters..."*
Isa. 35:7 (YLT)

During my entire nineteen years of pastoral service, I had never confronted anything as sinister as I did the summer of 2004. It became the most pivotal and life changing time in my life. Jesus confronted a system that I had carefully constructed. It was a system of busyness, professionalism, duty and all about the business of doing church. Our well-intentioned system, that I had a part in constructing, had taken a community of people away from the true meaning of church and the presence of God. Like the story in Kings where David desires to bring God's presence, by way of the Ark of the Covenant, back to Jerusalem, we had fallen into the same deception. David set about to do something wonderful for his people and for the Lord. The result was that one of David's devout men died a sudden and tragic death. David's heart was so troubled toward God while he tried to find understanding and meaning. Ultimately, David realized that he had not inquired of God as to what God wanted. David marched out on his own orders and God was not pleased. God wants us to do things His way. The second time David brought the Ark of the Covenant to Jerusalem, he read the word of God and carried the Ark of the Covenant with reverence as the Israelites in the wilderness had been taught to carry it. God was then very pleased and His presence was at the house where David placed the ark. You will read about the same harsh lesson we are learning today. Looking into the Bible as a mirror, we see ourselves like David, with a heart toward God but missing Him altogether. These are the accounts and lessons God has brought us to, and brought us through while we have been learning to seek God and do things His way.

There are many leaders in the church who are being visited with the knowledge that we have led the church in a way that has brought us to barrenness, religious blindness, and narcissism. In my quest to learn about how we got where we are, I found that the diagnosis is something that many in the church community agree upon; the church, particularly in America, is in desperate need of help. However, many, if not most, of the answers prescribe the same thing that got us to this condition; a program based approach. The following testimony does not offer a program or a plan with three easy-to-use steps to recovery. It is the unexpected encounter with He who is the One who said, *"I will build My church."* It is also an honest look at my own heart, which was in desperate need of

Desperate People in Desperate Times

being tenderized by the Great Shepherd's rod and merciful love and grace. I heard a message about the condition of the church at a meeting I attended on August 5, 2004. I remember the day well because my whole world changed. This was a direct message from God of which He would accept no excuses – no backing away – the conviction laid heavily upon my heart. God was not after my ministry. He was not even after the church where I was pastor. He was after me! The journey was, and is to this day, a journey that requires that I remain secure in Jesus and not in myself.

God was requiring things from me along my journey that were not logical. They were not things one would expect to see in a present-day church growth manual. Jesus would require that I acknowledge and say things publically that I am sure would be discouraged by most church leadership of our day. The elders and I dismantled program after program all in obedience to what we heard Jesus saying to us. There were many tests along the way, and we did not get a passing grade on them all. The grace and favor of Jesus was with us even in our failures because we had put the proverbial Ark of the Covenant back and started over doing things God's way. We had a new collective heart to obey.

The late Charles Finney spoke this;

> *"In breaking up your fallow ground, you must remove every obstruction. Things may be left that you think little things, and you may wonder why you do not feel as you wish to feel in religion, when the reason is that your proud and carnal mind has covered up something which God required you to confess and remove. Break up all the ground and turn it over. Do not bulk it, as the farmers say; do not turn it aside for little difficulties; drive the plough right*

INTRODUCTION

through them, beam deep, and turn the ground all up, so that it may all be mellow and soft, and fit to receive the seed and bear fruit a hundred fold."[1]

Our journey has been one of breaking up fallow ground. The rewards for what Charles Finney calls, "little difficulties," and for our honest evaluation and obedience, have been great. My prayer is that God will turn the ground in the church of America, and that we would once again bear the fruit for which God has planted us. ✝

INTRODUCTION ENDNOTES
1. Charles G. Finney, Breaking Up the Fallow Ground Online Sermons *www.Christiansunite.com/article 579*

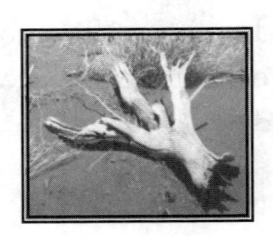

Chapter One

IT MATTERS NOT WHAT
BRINGS YOU TO DESPERATION

"...but Jacob replied, 'I will not let you go unless me you bless me.'"

It was for fear that Jacob cried out, *"I will not let you go unless you bless me."* What a mess of things he had made. Now he would have to face his brother, Esau, the next day. Esau, by all appearances, had prepared himself an army of men to take his rightful vengeance out upon the one who had stolen his inheritance. All of Jacob's usual manipulating, deceiving and lying would not spare him. Jacob would have to reckon for what he had done.

The Promise

"The Lord said to her (Rebekah), "Two nations are in your womb, and two peoples from within you will be separated; one people will be stronger than the other, and the older will serve the younger" *(Gen. 25:23 parentheses mine).*

It Matters Not What Brings You to Desperation

Why, when the Creator of the universe has promised a certain outcome, would the mother who *heard* the words, manipulate circumstances to try to help God with His desired outcome? Is God not capable of keeping His promises all on His own?

> *"Rebekah said to her son Jacob, 'Look, I overheard your father say to your brother Esau, "Bring me some game and prepare me some tasty food to eat, so that I may give you my blessing in the presence of the Lord before I die." 'Now, my son, listen carefully and do what I tell you: Go out to the flock and bring me two choice young goats, so that I can prepare some tasty food for your father, just the way he likes it. Then take it to your father to eat, so that he may give you his blessing before he dies.' Jacob said to his mother, 'But my brother is a hairy man, and I'm a man with smooth skin. What if my father touches me? I would appear to be tricking him and would bring down a curse on myself rather than a blessing.' His mother said to him, 'My son let the curse fall on me. Just do what I say, go and get them for me.' She also covered his hands and the smooth part of his neck with the goatskin."* (Gen. 27:6-13, 16)

This amazingly elaborate plot was concocted in an unnecessary effort to help God fulfill the destiny that He had already planned for Jacob. Jacob is not innocent in this conniving, by any means! He was dedicated to his mother's plot and complicit in the arranging of the details. Earlier Jacob had taken advantage of a situation when Esau came in from work, famished. Jacob insisted that Esau trade his birthright for food (Gen. 25:32).

Later, when Esau went into his father, Isaac, he discovered that Jacob had received the blessing of the firstborn son. Esau was furious. *"He took my birthright, and now he's taken my blessing! Esau held a grudge against Jacob...the days of my father are near; then I will kill my brother Jacob"* (Gen. 27:41).

Desperate People in Desperate Times

Jacob fled for his life to Paddan Aram; and after being away from home for many years, Jacob brought his herds, servants, and wives back to his homeland. The way Jacob and his mother had deceived Isaac and Esau, are we not surprised that Esau came to meet him with four hundred men? Fear gripped Jacob and caused him to fall to his knees before God as there was no other way for him to save his own life but that God would spare him. What do we do when we are desperate? We cry out to God until God answers. Jacob stayed awake all night and wrestled with the angel of the Lord for assurance that he would receive what he needed. Fear brought Jacob to a place of being desperate and the Lord honored him.

What brings us to this place of desperation does not seem to matter. What matters and what attracts God are those who are desperate for Him – those who have come to the end of themselves. We realize that without God, we are doomed, and we know that there is no other source for our salvation except that we refocus and surrender our entire lives to Him.

The dictionary's definition of the word — **Desperate:**
1. Reckless or violent because of despair; driven to take any risk. **2.** Undertaken as a last resort. **3.** Nearly hopeless; critical; grave **4.** Marked by, arising from, or showing despair; *despairing: the desperate look of hunger.* **5.** In an unbearable situation because of need or anxiety. **6.** Extreme because of fear, danger, or suffering. (*Webster's New Collegiate Dictionary*, p. 308)

We see clearly that Jacob's situation had become desperate! Jacob's life was marked by these circumstances. As we read the chapters of the Bible with the stories of Jacob's life, it is easy to see the decisions that took Jacob away from God and toward a selfish end. In my own reading through Jacob's

It Matters Not What Brings You to Desperation

history, I found myself giving counsel. I would say, "You have a great cause Jacob. Going after the promise of God is a good thing, but you are working so diligently doing the wrong things. Your intentions may be well, but your methods are getting you into trouble!" Oddly enough, the counsel that I received concerning *my own leadership* in the church where God had placed me was similar.

I had been laboring for many years under the misguided notion that if it was going to happen, it was up to me. All of the demographic studies, needs analyses, gift surveys, programs, charting, vision casting that I had done were all very sophisticated ways of bringing me to the same end as Jacob. These were clever methods I used in what I considered *my* ministry to do the business of God. I am not alone in my Jacob-like condition as God is showing us that the American church is in the midst of a cosmic clash of two wisdoms – God's and the world's. By the world's standards and by outward appearances, it seemed like we were succeeding and all was well. We had new buildings, new programs and people were busy all the time. God, in His sovereign plan, was at work to create a meeting place where I would be fired as the project coordinator for His business! As in the days of Jacob, God was demonstrating to me that if all I have to employ is man's wisdom, man's cleverness and man's knowledge that ultimately, it will never be enough. It would never be His church – and I would fail at the very ministry goals I felt led by God to accomplish.

Desperate Times in the Church

When we look at the condition of the church in America, most would agree that she has become a marginalized minority in our culture. When the world looks at us, it is not with desire because we have something that they do not have or because we are the picture of integrity, morality and honesty in our respective communities. The best surveys suggest that the church participates with the world in all that it has to offer rather than being separate from it. We have invested millions of dollars in fine edifices, soft padded pews, worship teams that sing the latest songs and programs that promise continued growth. Even if the programs delivered all that they promise, is it what the New Testament promises for the overcoming church in the earth?

There has been no substantial growth in the overall number of people who attend church in our city. Ten years ago a study showed that less than ten percent of the population of the citizens of Council Bluffs, Iowa attended church on a regular basis. Today, that statistic remains the same. These things hardly mattered to us as we kept ourselves ultra busy rolling out new programs and outreaches in the community. For the past ten years, we at Victory Fellowship had built a new facility to house all our growing needs in anticipation of all that we were hoping to accomplish for God. As we did this, we also expanded our programs and participated in every outreach in our community of which we could subscribe. All of which promised the same thing – growth; and all of it succeeding in keeping us very distracted from the fact that God was calling us to none of these things.

The Diagnosis

We *could* say that the condition of the inside of the church *is a direct result* of the condition on the outside of the church.

It Matters Not What Brings You to Desperation

In other words, the problem is out there, in the world that has lost its way. We could make excuses that people just don't want Jesus anymore because there is too much depravity. If we have concluded that the problem is the condition of the world, then we might deduce that the lure of the world is what is drawing people away from the church and God. We would then come to the only real solution: work harder and do a better job at creating more programs to attract people, i.e. entertainment, give-a-ways, crusades, etc.

We became desperate; desperate to do good things in the community and reach the lost and hurting people in the community. I was listening to my training that taught me to work harder and more creatively—and I did. Our church had experienced an immense appearance of growth in the years that my wife, Carolyn and I had served there. We established a Christian School and set up a college level training program to help disciple people and train them for ministry. We had purchased fourteen acres of ground and proceeded to build yet another new facility, which we had just begun to use, a few months before the elders and I began to sense in our spirits that something was missing. With all this growth, we had no sense of accomplishment. We all knew that something was desperately wrong and God was not pleased with what we had considered success! The issue for me was not moral failure or doctrinal error. It was much more sinister than that. I had assumed, through my every day routine of studying, visiting, managing, administrating, and program building, that God's presence was automatically with me. After all, I was a pastor – doing pastoral things – and being as responsible as all of my own energy and will could muster. Unfortunately, as good as my intentions may have been, God was not impressed. God was not in them, and I certainly had never surrendered and given Him the lead.

As important as all of my actions seemed to be in my own mind – God was as far from them as He was from Jacob as he manipulated circumstances to help God get to His desired outcome. All of the leaders of our church had become "Rebekah-minded." Somewhere along the way, we had substituted the *business* of ministry for His presence, preaching pop psychology instead of the Word of the Lord, and we had created a way to measure success that was focused on ministry as a business in corporate America.

Perhaps I had misinterpreted something in my training. I felt that if the Lord loved me, which I believe He does, He would *automatically* give me His favor. Given this favor, everything that I do for Him will automatically be successful. Success, I interpreted as growth and prosperity. Therefore, if we were not growing and prospering, I sank into despair wondering what was wrong. This is one of the sources of the massive depression seen among church leaders today. They are doing, doing, doing and it is never enough because the focus is not with the appropriate priorities. God woke us up in time, but it was a long road to realizing God's will and moving in it, versus continuing with our own will and asking God to bless us anyway!

A Different Diagnosis

On Thursday, August 5, 2004, the Heartland House of Prayer in Council Bluffs hosted a conference with a speaker by the name of Rhonda Hughey. I remember the date so very well as it was the day when God spoke my name as He did Jacob's. Rhonda's message was a call to the church to consider who's lead they are following:

> "The current condition of the church suggests that we have replaced the purity and simplicity of the gospel with sophisticated, entertaining activities that have left people inside and outside the community of faith questioning the reality of Jesus Christ and His life-changing power...The western church is struggling with her identity, authority, and purpose. Understanding our true identity in Christ must occur before we can exercise spiritual authority and accomplish our God-given mission as an agent of change in the earth...God is challenging the church's self-centered identity and shifting our mindsets and ineffective methodologies. He is inviting us to respond to one of the greatest challenges we have ever faced – to return to our first love and to step out of our compromised church culture into His kingdom!" [1]

This encounter became a divine wake-up call for our church. Every leader of Victory Fellowship who was at this meeting heard it, and we all knew we were hit with a truth from God that required immediate action. Thus began our quest, and we had no idea how to proceed with change. We set out to recover our desire for our First Love, the One we had left and did not even realize it. We did not realize, at the time, that we had just surrendered ourselves to a long and arduous journey that would land us right where we wanted to be – at the very heart and presence of the Head of the Church: Jesus!

The rest of this book is not just a story of my personal struggles and change, or just the journey of our leadership team and the congregation. It is also the story of the progress in our community to see such wide-spread transformation because of our newfound focus on God's presence and our intimacy with Him alone. It is a message of hope for the American Church.

Our transformation was not founded on my wisdom and ingenuity, but it is based on Heaven's response to hearts that are crying out to Jesus for Him to help us restore God's presence in all that we do.

The message that God brought to us through Rhonda Hughey led us into a wilderness experience. We endured this dry, humbling season for the purpose of reorienting us to His presence. In this season, God would show us much of which we needed to repent. We also would learn that what the Lord wanted was for the human-devised elaborate system of doing church business to die.

It had become very comfortable for us to be in this place as it was non-threatening to the strongholds in the city. God began replacing our ways with His own. Next to my conversion experience, this wilderness experience has been the most challenging, disorienting, confusing and priority altering time in my life.

When this journey began, I had been a Christian all of my adult life, and I had been active in leadership in this growing church for more than twenty years. This experience showed me the wretchedness of myself. What hurt most of all, was realizing how far from God's will I had traveled in my pursuit of growth and perfection. I was perfectly wrong, but God saw into my heart and my eagerness to please Him. He saw how much I truly loved Him, but was lost in the messy system. After coming through this experience, I must say, this has been the most uncomfortable time of my life, and yet I know in my spirit that it was well worth the investment as God led us all the way through it and onto the right path with Jesus rightly at the helm. There is no greater feeling for a surrendered Christian than to realize you are directly in God's will and that He is genuinely pleased with you. This is not only a place of great satisfaction, as we are all created to be one with God, but it is also a great position of power as we walk closely with God with Jesus leading the way. ✝

CHAPTER ONE ENDNOTES
1. Rhonda Hughey, "Desperate for His Presence" Bethany House Publishers 2004, 14

Personal Journal Entry
August 9, 2004

"For the time has come for judgment to began at the house of God." 1 Peter 4:17.

"...the judgments of the Lord are true and righteous altogether, more to be desired are they then gold...sweeter also than honey and the honeycomb, moreover by them your servant is weaned and in keeping them is great reward" Psalm 19:9.

I have never felt the judgment of God on my heart like I do now. It is a very fearful thing...I feel disgusted with myself, my devotional life... everything! I am starting a fast today, and also feel I am to stop spending time studying and to just get alone with God. I feel the judgment of God on my life and I want to know how to consider them sweeter than honey.

God is leading me to a lot of verses that have to do with idolatry and He is pointing out things that are idolatrous in me that I had never considered. My desire and worship is so centered around accomplishments...I cannot believe that what brought me joy only a few days ago, I now am weeping over! I don't know what to do except repent.

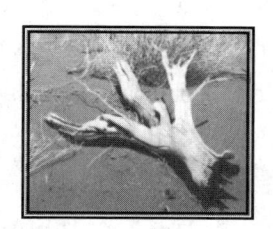

Chapter Two
DESPERATION MAKES YOU DO WHAT YOU WOULD NOT ORDINARILY DO
"The man asked him, 'What is your name?'
'Jacob,' he answered" (Gen. 32:27).

The reason for this question was not that the angel was having trouble remembering Jacob's name. It was to prompt Jacob into his own admission of guilt. It caused Jacob to express what he was and what he had become. It was also to bring about a change in Jacob's heart. God gave Jacob a new name, with a new destiny, but in order for this to happen, Jacob had to suffer the death of his first identity.

"Then the man asked, 'What is your name?' 'Jacob,' he answered. Then the man said, 'Your name will no longer be Jacob, but Israel, because you have struggled with God and with man and have overcome'" (Gen. 32:27-28).

Earlier in this passage of Scripture, we read how Jacob was blessed. He was arriving back home with so much after

Desperate People in Desperate Times

leaving with so little. Yet, there was still an inward knowing and an inward gnawing that something was very wrong. When we have hostility between siblings (even in God's kingdom), the air is never clear until we deal with the situation, which is why God tells us that He doesn't even want our offerings until we settle disputes between brothers and sisters (blood and kingdom related). Our minds are never at peace until we make things right, especially when we are the guilty party. Jacob had built on a shaky foundation, and there was a real threat that he could lose it all very quickly. There needed to be a deep restructuring of his foundation from the unrighteous to the righteous, and Jacob knew it. This sense in his spirit brought him to a place of understanding and recognizing his own total desperation.

Testing Foundations

Even when there is apparent success, God will challenge and test what sort of stuff we build upon. As long as the source of our building is from the old man's strength, wisdom, and our own creativity, it will not stand through the test of fire. Paul reminds the church of an important promise, a promise of fire that will test our building materials. *"For no one can lay any foundation other than the one already laid, which is Jesus Christ. If any man builds on this foundation using gold, silver, costly stones, wood, hay or straw, his work will be shown for what it is, because the Day will bring it to light. It will be revealed with fire, and the fire will test the quality of each man's work." (1 Cor. 3:11-13).*

It is easy, expedient and inexpensive to build with wood, hay and straw but those building materials will not stand up to the test of God's fire. Building God's church with inadequate materials equates to building with human ingenuity, wisdom and creativity. The building will not last. Building with gold, silver and costly stones provides the opposite – or what symbolizes the wisdom and direction of God – the building that will last even through the fire. It takes much longer to build with these materials, but even when the wait seems long past what seems to be rational, we know that God is giving the orders and the direction. Our goal is to serve Him and to do things God's way to provide a permanent and lasting foundation for the church.

Paul goes on to remind us that provision from the Lord is not necessarily an indication of His approval. Using Israel in the wilderness as an example; *"They all ate the same spiritual food, and drank the same spiritual drink; for they drank from the spiritual rock that accompanied them, and that rock was Christ. Nevertheless, God was not pleased with most of them; their bodies were scattered over the desert"* (1 Cor. 10:3-5). This is a very important truth for us to understand as we, who are genuinely surrendered to Christ, end up on this journey of abandoning self will. The journey leads us on to find God's will for whatever destiny He has in store for our lives. It would have been very easy for us to conclude that, since we were experiencing some measure of success in our church, that God must have been pleased with us. It was not so! We had only been experiencing the amazing *mercy* that God has for His people. As I stated before, God did give us a small degree of success for the benefit of the people in our congregation in spite of our misdirected and inept leadership tactics. God protected His people while He brought us to this pertinent place of understanding and then, through the wilderness journey.

Personal Confrontation

After Rhonda Hughey revealed what God had shown her about the diagnosis of the church, she suggested that the prescription for our condition was the presence of Jesus.

> "Today it is rare to find a church where the manifest presence of Jesus is the primary attraction or sustained focus...It would appear that the corporate church today has made an erroneous conclusion – that her ministry is no longer absolutely dependent upon the evidential reality of Christ's presence. A theology of His abiding presence has replaced hunger for and the pursuit of His glorious manifest presence." [1]

Rhonda spoke about the manifest presence of Jesus in a way that I had never considered, distinguishing manifest presence from omnipresence. Suddenly it hit me; most of the programs we were doing in the church, we had presumed upon His manifest presence. We simply assumed that any program that we imported from someone else's ministry would bring the same glory to ours.

As Rhonda spoke to us, she followed the course of the typical church in America and about the logical conclusions of our choices. What she described was our church.

> "We have many methods and plans about how to make people feel welcome in the church. Many of those methods are successful in drawing people, but are they drawing the presence of the Lord? The presence of Jesus always has been and always will be what is most attractive for hungry people. For long-term success, we must build something that attracts His presence.
>
> "When God's presence becomes a tangible reality in a community, the church then becomes a catalyst for growth. God's presence is more effective than our best church growth methods. When God's presence is tangible, spiritual ministry results and becomes a magnet for hungry souls and broken people." [2]

Jesus, Himself had said in *John 12:32, "But, I, when I am lifted up from the earth, will draw all men to myself."* We had forgotten the importance of this, and the way back, Rhonda explained, was first through repentance, and then to ask Jesus to restore His presence back to His church. His presence was the ultimate ingredient for the church's solid foundation. As our hearts were restored and our minds opened to the freshness of her message from God, we understood this to be a pivotal moment for our church – and for our entire lives. There are times in our lives that we identify as pivotal moments. Jacob had identified his pivotal moment as he wrestled with the Lord. God had come close to Jacob that night to give him the opportunity to turn from *his* selfish ways and follow God.

God was approaching my heart and mind in the same way. This was my "Jacob moment." I knew that it was time to change my direction, and the experience was both fearful and wonderful. It was fearful because it brought me to the realization of my situation and to see my real self. There was no loud music, no strong invitation loaded with enticing words to draw me to the altar. We received a simple invitation to come forward, followed by a simple, yet life-changing and powerful prayer of repentance.

I had not known the tug of the Lord upon my heart for such a long, long time. That night I nearly crawled to the altar to lay my heart bare before God in repentance. I had always presumed Jesus was with us, but I had not been about the Father's business of asking for His presence or intentionally lifting Jesus up. I felt a weight upon me. It was a heavy weight of the responsibility for the inept leadership I had exercised toward God's own church — His people! I could not really say much at all; through the hot tears of sorrow upon my face, I managed a heartfelt and genuine prayer of repentance. The atmosphere in the place that night was heavy with conviction. The Holy Spirit was at work, revealing God's truth in all who were present. A quiet reverence rested in the sanctuary as people lingered, weeping at the altar. God's people were finally hungry for Him, and this is what He had always wanted from us. For several moments, everyone present understood the inappropriateness of speech. There were no words to communicate what was in our hearts as we just sat in a room filled with the manifest presence of Jesus. It would take me a very long time to work out language for the changes that were happening, a longer time still to determine how this would affect the ministry in our church.

Wrestling With Presence

Victory Fellowship Church was not atypical of any other church in America. We were diligently working to draw people to God and to our church. Admittedly, the primary way our church was growing was through transfer growth. People, for one reason or another, left other churches to join us.

My family and I have served Victory Fellowship since 1986 and since that time, there has not been a change in the overall percentage of people who regularly attend church in the city. That fact had not stopped us from creating elaborate programs for the nursery to the adults in order to keep them excited and energized about what was happening at Victory! The last thing that any of us in leadership had on our mind was dismantling anything. You know the old adage: "If it is

Desperation Makes You Do...

not broke, don't fix it!" We believed that sensationalism was what brought the numbers and filled our quota for membership, but this message we heard about the hunger for the presence of Jesus told us that something was indeed broke. We sensed that something was disjointed, but we just would not stop long enough to notice it or even to hear God within the confines of our own high-energy meetings. We were hungry, but hungry for the wrong thing. We were so busy with the business of church that we did not stop long enough to hear that small, still voice of God. We were as guilty as Jacob and his mother, Rebekah, of conspiring to help God out with what He had promised. God then asked us to come with Him on an adventure into the unknown.

God was asking us to make a decision to leave the very predictable world that we had carefully constructed to go to a place where He was Lord and would lead us, not day by day, but step by step. God brought us to a place where He would turn us inside out and show us what we had become. We knew in our spirit that the Lord was speaking, but we sincerely had no idea what to do next, but felt the loving hand of the Lord present with us. This was our wrestling period with the Lord. We wanted something desperately from the Lord — Him — and He was not as quick to answer as we had expected. We learned quickly to set aside our expectations and wait on God and His timing.

For the next several elder meetings, when the other four elders and I would meet, we ceremonially put all of our programs and agendas on the table and asked the Lord to remove anything that was not from Him. God first began to speak to our hearts about our own leadership in the church – each of our strengths and our weaknesses. My leadership style was heavy on structure and predictability. I had kept things in the church pretty constructed. We heard the Lord say, *"I will build My church and the gates of hell will not prevail against it"* (Matt. 16:18). I realized that there were some things that I had missed in my Bible study regarding this revelation that had been spoken to the Apostle Peter.

First, unlike Jacob and Rebekah, we all realized that God is perfectly capable of fulfilling His promises with or without our help. The important thing for us was to do our part and step back to allow Jesus to fill His role. Second, when Jesus is the architect of His church, the gates of hell will not overpower the church. *"Unless the LORD builds the house, They labor in vain who build it; Unless the LORD guards the city, The watchman keeps awake in vain"* (Ps. 127:1 NASB).

As in the days of the early church, the leaders stayed in a place of constant prayer, fasting and worship *until* the Holy Spirit spoke His instructions; He would accompany their efforts. *"In the church at Antioch there were prophets and teachers...While they were worshiping the Lord and fasting, the Holy Spirit said, 'Set apart for me Barnabas and Saul for the work to which I have called them.' So after they had fasted and prayed, they placed their hands on them and sent them out"* (Acts 13:1-3). Hearing from the Lord was so important that even after they all agreed that they were to send Barnabas and Saul, they entered back into a time of prayer and fasting, presumably for more specific direction from the Holy Spirit. The next verse goes on to say that, *"The two of them, sent on their way by the Holy Spirit..."* There is another clue about what the Holy Spirit was revealing to this company in verse forty-seven:

Desperation Makes You Do...

"For this is what the Lord commanded us: 'I have made you a light to the Gentiles..." The Holy Spirit had some very distinct instructions for them. I believe that the Holy Spirit still has some very specific instructions for those who will wait with the same attitude of prayer, fasting and worship.

We were beginning to see a very important guiding principle from the Lord. His presence will lead, and as His word in the Bible also indicates, His presence will hold us back if we will listen. Later, as Paul continued his travels, he was forbidden to preach in certain areas and, in a dream, God gave him specific instruction for ministry.

"Now when they had gone through Phrygia and the region of Galatia, they were forbidden by the Holy Spirit to preach the word in Asia. After they had come to Mysia, they tried to go into Bithynia, but the Spirit did not permit them. So passing by Mysia, they came down to Troas. And a vision appeared to Paul in the night. A man of Macedonia stood and pleaded with him, saying, 'Come over to Macedonia and help us.' Now after he had seen the vision, immediately we sought to go to Macedonia, concluding that the Lord had called us to preach the gospel to them" (Acts 16:6-10). The guiding factor in the early church that we had overlooked, again I reiterate, was *His manifest presence*. What evidence did we have that the Lord's presence was with us as we were building buildings and constructing new programs? Certainly none like they evidenced in the early church. The better question: When was the last time we had denied our fleshly desires to do something, anything and simply stopped and waited on the Lord for instruction? We were not only trying to find the right answers, but the right questions for God as well. The truth is, we had run so far ahead of the

Lord, we had no specific direction from the Lord concerning most of the things we were doing. We assumed that because we were doing good things that the presence of the Lord would accompany us. The stakes were way too high for us to continue on presuming we had the presence of the Lord. The lesson about the early church leaders posturing themselves before the Lord in prayer before setting their course in ministry was a very new thing for all of us in leadership at Victory Fellowship.

Learning to Hear Jesus' Voice

A road map would have been really nice right at about this time. The elders continued to try to navigate through the many questions that had come up. We all agreed that the Lord was convicting us about the foundation that we had built upon. We had allowed ourselves to be swept up in treating our ministry like a business venture. Victory Fellowship had become a very good marketer for – you guessed it – Victory Fellowship! I wish that I could say that our motives were to market the gospel as that would sound a little better, but it would not be true. We even designed our evangelism and outreach strategies to make a good impression, and hopefully, to get a few more people in *our* church. None of these things were birthed out of a place of prayer!

Some unforeseen problems began when we started talking and praying about how to redo our shaky foundation. Jesus confronted Victory Fellowship with fire to test what sort of foundation we had built upon. When we began to realize what this meant, it was not setting very well with everyone. Patience was required at this important juncture. We had to have patience with each other as each person readjusted their priorities and fought past the fear so that they could see Jesus as being the center importance. We had to have patience as we waited for a word from the Lord to get us started. We knew how wrong we had been, and we were afraid to move forward without a direct word from Him.

The congregation had to have patience with us as Jesus redirected, and all of the built-in comfort zones were removed. We endured many trials while learning to live and love each other through these difficult times. Much trust was required that God was leading and that the leadership was under the direct hand of God as we reversed our large engines and stopped. To proceed in a forward momentum, we had to come to a complete stop first. In order to go in the right direction, we had to wait on God or we would have been in the same situation once again – headed off, full keel, without God.

After we ceremonially placed all of the programs and agendas on the altar and asked the Lord to remove anything that was not from Him, things began to happen. It took a couple of weeks, but Jesus began to speak to our hearts. Our situation was worse than any of us had suspected. Jesus began to show us our motives for doing what we were doing. Again, I began to feel the full weight of responsibility for the leadership of the church. This time, I was not alone as the men who sat around that table felt it as well. We were crying out for God to forgive us and for the way we had been leading His church. There were broken and contrite hearts in the men and women who had led alongside me. This sincere attitude of our hearts led us directly to total repentance. If we were to stop everything we did that was out of a selfish motive – any motive that was not from the Lord, we felt that we would nearly be at a standstill. So slowly, over a period of weeks we stopped many of the programs and began to pray about the way we were administrating the church's activities. We simply tried to wait on the Lord and listen for Jesus to teach us what to do. When He saw our broken and contrite hearts toward Him, He led us in God's ways so that we would realize His presence and know God's approval every step of the way. ☦

Chapter Two Endnotes
1. Rhonda Hughey, "Desperate for His Presence" Bethany House Publishers 2004, 34
2. Ibid., 32

Personal Journal Entry
September 2, 2004

Wait for the Lord; be strong and take heart and wait for the Lord. Ps. 27:14

I will wait for the Lord, who is hiding His face from the house of Jacob. I will put my trust in Him. Isa. 8:17

Truly you are a God who hides Himself, O God and Savior of Israel. Isa. 45:15

Demands of life scream at me not to wait... The offer that Satan made to Jesus was to rule over the kingdoms of the earth if He would worship him. It was an offer that would be a shortcut to Jesus' ultimate position. It was a shortcut to ruling (which Jesus would do anyway as God had planned it) – but the catch was that Jesus would be in submission to Satan!

September 7, 2004

The noise of the world is like anesthesia that deadens our pain, drowns out the voice of God and blinds us to the needs of others.

Chapter Three

God Speaks to Desperate People

*"...Your name will no longer be Jacob,
but Israel, because you have struggled with God
and with men and have overcome"* (Gen. 32:27).

A new beginning was exactly what Jacob needed. His given name had stuck with him, and he had carried out the prophetic meaning of that name, "deceiver and supplanter." God was the crew chief in charge of this nature change that would make this man, a man worthy of carrying the name of God's chosen people: Israel. A legal change of name, though expensive, is relatively easy today. To change the nature of an individual is not so easy. What we often overlook in this nature change in Jacob is the word, *"struggled,"* which is synonymous with the word *"suffered!"* Jacob's metamorphosis did not come easy. It came with a high price. That price was the struggle of breaking free from the seeming safety of control and predictability. It is interesting that God did not say a word about Jacob's deeds. There is no rebuke for his lies...no mention of any of it. Instead, God wanted an admission of guilt. Then, in the final exchange between God and Jacob, God rewards Jacob for this preliminary struggle with his new name: Israel. I am sure this made as much sense to Jacob as it did when Jesus walked up to Simon and said, *"Your name is Peter,"* or when the angel came to Gideon and called *him, "a mighty man of valor."* The distance between what these men were in reality and what God spoke over them, is the place of struggle and suffering. All God required from Jacob, Simon, and Gideon, or any of the rest of us, is a, *"yes,"* in agreement with Him. Agreement with God grants Him permission for Him to begin to work on our foundation.

Early Beginnings

It was in college when I first came into agreement with God on His call to the ministry. From that day, there was never any intent to deceive anyone. In that regard, the early years of Jacob's life were very different from mine. The Lord used Jacob's life, though, to show me that there were some very real similarities. From my first commission to pastor a small rural church in Iowa there was a "go" in my heart. With all my training and everything within me, I was ready, and more than willing. My wife and I quit our well-paying jobs, pulled up stakes in our urban lifestyle and moved to a very rural community. I remember the first visit by my mother and father-in-law to our new home – our place of beginning. We showed them around with some pride. First, we showed them the church; we walked up and moved the rock that helped hold the door closed. It had an oil-burning stove that sat in the middle of the sanctuary. Before each service, I would go in and light it an hour before it was time for the service to start. We did not have to worry about the water pipes freezing because there were none. The bathrooms were around the back, and, they were aptly called, "outhouses." Quite a disadvantage to church growth, I thought, but folks around this rural community did not blink an eye at the quaint amenities.

You should have seen my in-laws eyes when we showed them! The parsonage did have inside facilities – installed two years before we got there, hallelujah! You could actually look across our yard into a pasture full of long horned steers. Well, needless to say, Carolyn's parents did not make a long stay of it. They gave their blessing and quickly drove away.

That small community of thirty or so people had two churches. As it turns out, several years before we went there to pastor, there was a church split and thus, the creation of two churches in this small community. We did not let this hinder our efforts to bring them into the church. We hit the ground running!

Church growth is the result of hard work we were told. "Find a need and fill it," was also one of our favorite adages. My prayer life consisted of asking God to bless my efforts. We were giving our all because that is the way it was done. How could God resist blessing such sacrifices?

From the beginning of my ministry until August 5th of 2004, when I heard Rhonda Hughey speak God's truths at the Heartland House of Prayer in Council Bluffs, you could not tell me differently. The days following my encounter with the Lord at that small, but significant meeting, were filled with much needed change. My hardened heart was turned to flesh as God called me into this new understanding. This was my divine wake-up call.

Wrestling with the Lord

Almost immediately following this revelation in my life, God began to communicate with me about areas that needed work. Remember, God had begun showing us our strengths and weaknesses. It was time for God to work with me on my weak areas. The first area God wanted me to concentrate on had to do with how I spent my time. Jesus was calling me to just sit with Him, no studying to prepare for a service with elaborate power point presentations, just quietly sitting with my Bible and journal – learning to actually listen for His voice and know His presence.

Some of the things that the Lord showed me about me were alarming. Just as the case in Jacob's life, God was not revealing this to change the fruit, but to change the root. All that I could do was to repent. This went on for about six months. Almost daily, I would go into the church sanctuary – the same place every day – and wait and meditate. Daily, the Lord was confronting me with the things in my heart that no one wants to admit are there. Jesus was there to offend me... my flesh...my way of doing things.

How nice it would have been to have a retreat center to get away so that I could somehow approve this journey or learn it from a distance and then, come back with a nice packaged presentation for the leaders and the church. No, my journey was ugly and everybody in our fellowship got a front row seat to it.

There were days that everything God had to say was for me and no one else. Then there were things that were for or about His church. The Lord began to show me things about how I pastor His church. The heart of Jesus was revealed to me, and it stirred me so after I had been led to the passage in *Jer. 50:6: "My people have been lost sheep; their shepherds have led them astray and caused them to roam on the mountains. They wondered over mountain and hill and forgot their own resting place."* As you can imagine, my heart broke as I meditated on this, knowing that I had been one of those shepherds. I was guilty! As these words sank into my spirit, I became totally aware that much of my ministry leadership style had to change. I had touched the jealous heart of God and it was a terrifying thing. I will never want to stand before God and answer for the worldly ways and strategies that I had employed to lead His people. I was driven to the floor, to my knees, and then, completely prostrate before the convicting power of Almighty God. I was a lump of clay ready to be remade by His hand. Again, I found it very difficult to speak. My only thought was, *"O God, please give me another chance!"* If I was to be given another chance, I knew that I must repent before the very sheep I had been leading – God's sheep – the congregation of people who had entrusted me as their pastor.

Public Repentance

On that Sunday, when it came time for me to speak, I read this text from Jeremiah 50, and through the same repentant hot tears, I spoke to the people about all that God had dealt with me about. The same conviction that was with me a few days before, attended the words which I spoke that morning.

At the conclusion of my repenting, I asked God's people for forgiveness. I bowed my head and began to pray. I kept my eyes closed, afraid to open them. When I finished praying, I paused – keeping my eyes tightly closed. After a couple of moments, the silence was broken by the sound of a small child's voice. He was genuinely repenting for his own disobedience. I opened my eyes, and to my surprise, the majority of the church had joined me in the front, many of them weeping. The young boy's prayer of repentance opened the flood-gates for repentance that morning. I had expected quite a different reaction. My imagination ran away with me as I reviewed over and over again how I would do this. I truly thought that if I disclosed what was on my heart that morning, the people would no longer respect my leadership. It was while facing that mountain of fear that I spoke that morning. What happened was just the opposite of what I had imagined would happen.

The Lord required other course corrections for us. It seemed that many of our meetings together following this point, were filled with confession and repentance. I had always preached about the need for repentance, but never before been in so many services where people were compelled to repent! Because of my willingness to publicly repent, we had unintentionally, but wonderfully, created a safe environment for other people to follow. We became the sanctuary that God had intended for us to be. The leader does set the tone and the atmosphere in the church where they lead. Where the shepherd goes, the sheep will follow. God wanted His sheep led properly, and so He got my attention as a shepherd to start leading His sheep His way! Even though the elders, deacons, and other leaders and I knew that our decisions would have some negative effects on the attendance of the services, we knew that we were following the Lord in this journey. We also knew that when some decided to leave our fellowship that we would pray for their return, but we were not willing to alter our journey if that was the cost for them to stay. This was yet another test from the Lord. Would we continue to follow Jesus and bless those who would leave?

In an article by Art Katz entitled, <u>Pretext or Reality?,</u> he writes about the three tribes of Israel who decided to remain on the desert side of the Jordan River. *"...not all of the house of Israel crossed, but a portion of the tribes of Gad, Manasseh and Reuben chose to remain on the other side. They remained because the ground there was lush, and the grasses were high and they were cattle breeders, who obviously recognized something of immediate value. They were unwilling for that risk of a faith in what might be found on the other side.*

They pleaded with Moses and got what they wanted, and they were allowed to remain on the wrong side of the Jordan and have been subsequently lost to the whole history of Israel. The only melancholy reminder we have of the tribe of Gad, who chose the wrong side, are the Gadarenes of the New Testament time who raised pigs and were unwilling, even at a later time, for a deliverer to come because it proved expensive for the flesh. They much preferred to sustain their herds, rather than welcome Him who casting those same herds into the sea delivers from evil spirits!"[1]

What a commentary on the consequences of an unwillingness to cross over, of languishing on the wrong side. I think that the reason is always the same – because it is conducive to the 'flesh,' because back there we have an assurance of things that pertain to "herds," i.e., our immediate self-interest. It would be easy to go back to the old ways. It would seem to be the logical thing to do especially as our finances were shrinking and as families decided to worship elsewhere. This is the struggle, and it was a real struggle for us – the suffering that produced in us a new nature. As difficult as the journey was becoming, we decided not ever to turn back. Our ship was headed in a new direction with Jesus at the helm and we had no desire to be anywhere without God. We determined in our hearts to do things God's way, from that point forward.

Leaning on Jesus

It was a difficult and slow process, changing the way things had always been done. I am, like all humans, a creature of habit. I loved spending hours studying in preparation to preach. As I spoke of earlier, for a long period following our new beginning, my study and preparation time was sitting before the Lord with my Bible and a prayer journal – waiting on God. God then began challenging me to take my prayer journal to the pulpit – not my usual sermon notes. The first few times I followed this instruction were frightening. It became easier, over time, to pray and allow the Lord to speak His thoughts – then take God's thoughts to the congregation of the Lord. Jesus is a very good teacher and He desires to teach through His servants. As I began this practice, the time spent in solitude was very difficult, and the conviction that the Lord brought was confrontational to all that was normal to me. As I continued, my spiritual disciplines turned into an appetite. There are still times that it seems like God is nowhere to be found in my life, but when I touch heaven for a moment, it does not matter that I had to endure a season of drought. There was a metamorphosis going on in my heart. Everything about my passions, pleasures, and emotions were in a state of change. God was creating a new heart in me – a heart of genuine service toward Him and His people. ✝

> *"Create in me a clean heart, O God, And renew a steadfast spirit within me. Do not cast me away from Your presence, And do not take Your Holy Spirit from me. Restore to me the joy of Your salvation. And sustain me with a willing spirit"* (Ps. 51:10-12 NASB).

CHAPTER THREE ENDNOTES
1. Art Katz, Apostolic Conversion, Pretext or Reality?
    www.artkatzministries.org/apostolic-conversion/WordPress - Ad Clerum Entries (RSS) and Comments (RSS) Podcast Powered by podPress (v8.8)

Personal Journal Entry
August 12, 2004

"But seek first His kingdom and His righteousness and all these things will be given to you as well" Matt. 6:33.

As I was meditating on Matthew 6:33 today I felt Jesus say to me, "I know when you seek Me...and I know when you seek Me for things." An immediate conviction came over me as I know that most of my coming before Him is for things.

...then I looked...and saw an idol...And God said to me, do you see what they are doing – the utterly detestable things...that will drive Me far from my sanctuary?" Ezek. 8:5-6.

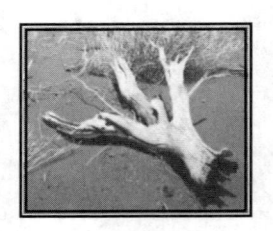

Chapter Four

THE DISTINGUISHING MARKS OF DESPERATE PEOPLE

"Then Jacob asked, saying, 'Tell me Your name, I pray.' And He said, 'Why is it that you ask about My name?' And He blessed him there. And Jacob called the name of the place Peniel: 'For I have seen God face to face, and my life is preserved,' Just as he crossed over Peniel the sun rose on him, and he limped on his hip" (Gen. 32:29-31 NKJV).

What would be a sign of Jacob's encounter with the Lord? It was not something that would be a secret between God and the man. No, it was much more conspicuous than that, a limp that would remain with him to the end of his life. *"By faith Jacob, when he was dying, blessed each of the sons of Joseph, and worshiped, leaning on the top of his staff"* Heb. 11:21 (NKJV). Understanding that the list of people in Hebrews is God's Hall of Faith, Jacob's name made it into this list, but he made it while limping! God breaks down our flesh so that we will walk in faith with Him.

The Distinguishing Marks of Desperate People

Jacob's life had undergone a name change, which would represent the nature changes that were under way. Jacob's experience, in the presence of God, resulted in a physical manifestation as well reminding him of his continual need to lean on God. Out of necessity, Jacob's life changed because of his God-inflicted injury. Some might look on this affliction as humiliating. For Jacob, it was a souvenir from Peniel when God came so close to him that he won His favor.

Like Jacob's souvenir from Peniel, the Apostle Paul also carried an annoyance or disability in his body and sought the Lord to remove it. The Lord told Paul that His strength is made perfect in our weakness and that His grace would be sufficient for Paul to carry him during his ministry. After Jesus spoke this revelation to Paul, Paul said, *"If that is the case, I will boast in my infirmities and weaknesses"* (2 Cor. 12:7-9 paraphrased). The object of both Paul and Jacob's suffering was a continual reminder that God's strength would uphold them, always. The object of our boasting at Victory Fellowship was our carefully constructed and organized programs. I had gone to great lengths to study the latest trends and target our resources for maximum impact. I had attended many seminars and conferences of successful leaders and pastors over the years and was very confident in what we were doing. We were holding our own, right up there with the best and biggest of all the conglomerate churches. One of the most amazing things I had to learn was that I could no longer lean on imported programs and someone else's great ideas. I had gotten no word from the Lord for any specific thing that I had implemented. We just dropped programs that didn't work and moved on to the next one if the first did not prove to be as successful as advertised.

Desperate People in Desperate Times

A New Leadership Style

In all my education, I had never had a single lesson on how to wait on the Lord. Up to this time in my ministry, the goal of each day was to move through my routine of scheduled events, meetings and calls. Serving the Lord meant mostly serving people's needs and requests. My leadership style was undergoing a dramatic change! Waiting was and is becoming a major requirement for me in order to hear the voice that must guide, the voice of Jesus. What I was finding is that waiting is one of the most remarkable ways that Jesus uses in leading His people.

The very thing that broke the back of King Saul's leadership in Israel was his impatient heart. He simply could not wait at Gilgal for the prophet Samuel to offer a sacrifice to the Lord before the army went into battle. The army was getting impatient and began to scatter, thus Saul began to fear and did not continue to wait for the proper sequence of events as God had commanded. When Saul walked out of obedience and offered the sacrifice himself, Samuel said this to King Saul; *"You have not kept the command the Lord your God gave you; if you had, he would have established your kingdom over Israel for all time. But now your kingdom shall not endure; the Lord has sought out a man after his own heart and appointed him leader of his people, because you have not kept the Lord's command"* (1 Sam. 13:13-14).

On the other hand, we see David's heart, the man after God's own heart – a man who was used to waiting and placed value on waiting for the Lord. As we read in his Psalm, David states the importance of waiting, *"Wait on the Lord: and be of good courage and He shall strengthen thy heart, wait I say, on the Lord"* (Ps. 27:14). Patience or waiting is not a very popular subject among believers, yet the Bible gives considerable attention to this virtue. A synonym for one of the Hebrew words for *wait* is to *trust.* The issue for King Saul was an issue of lack of trust in the Lord, which manifested itself in his haste. I am also fully convinced that the only way we learn this kind of waiting on God is by doing it. He teaches us to grow in patience, faith and trust.

Learning to Wait

Jesus began to challenge my impatience as He was calling me into a new level of trusting Him. Typically, my desire was for a predictable and structured service. When Jesus is lifted up, and becomes the center of the service experience, it tends to mess up scheduled events and structure. For people who are used to the component of control, this was a bit overwhelming. When this first began to happen in 2004, God gave me a big dose of the fruit of the spirit called, *"self control."* It was difficult to sit back and wait for Jesus to lead. The services began to take a new shape as we followed the lead of the Holy Spirit. We began to meet at 9:00 a.m. for a half hour of prayer before service. This soon turned into a full hour that led right into the praise and worship time. We spent more time in worship and prayer during the service, and often during the worship time, people would move to the front and kneel or lie down on the floor near the altar. There would be times of silence as we all prayed, waiting and listening for the Lord.

If the reward of my waiting is something that I really want, then waiting is tolerable. However, if for my waiting the real conditions of my heart are exposed, then that is another thing indeed. Conditions became conducive in this atmosphere created by the Holy Spirit, to expose such things as pride, suspicion, a competitive spirit, ambition, and comparison. In as much as these malignancies are present in me, I must learn to lean on the Lord's grace for His antidote.

It seemed that Jesus had allowed me to taste His goodness so that I would want more. I became desperate for the presence of Jesus. The next thing that I encountered was my own compromised heart. For all of my seeking Him, I expected more of the sweetness of what I previously experienced. Instead, He continually held up that wretched mirror to let me see my own wretched heart. There was only one thing I could do about this, again!. Repent... again! The repentance continues to this day as Jesus continues to test my heart. He keeps that full-length mirror in front of me as He promises in His Word. These times of reflection keep me genuine and honest toward Him and others about the condition of my heart. There is such a tendency in me to return to presumption and programming. Presumption always makes us vulnerable to the enemy and takes us away from the Lord's presence. We must continually practice waiting on direction from the Lord.

Posturing Our Hearts

At this juncture in our journey, it would have been easy to clap our hands in praise for what He has done and move on. We had previously been so caught in the trap of expecting the Lord to instantly respond to our whims, but He was not so quick to respond to our tears and cries. At times, He has been disappointingly slow. While He continued to bring His comfort, it seemed the Lord wanted us to learn to posture ourselves in such a way – a better way – and this would be our default position. I do not know if I'll ever understand His ways in this completely, I am sure that not too many of us do, but David's words offer some help. *"How long O Lord, will you forget me forever? How long will you hide your face from me? How long must I wrestle with my thoughts and every day sorrow in my heart?...But I will trust in your unfailing love; my heart rejoices in your salvation"* (Ps. 13:1-2, 5).

Apparently, David was experiencing such a place in his relationship with the Lord where he simply had to trust, wait, and lean on the promise of the Lord's faithfulness as he continued to pursue God. The Lord loves to be sought after. He loves when we pare away distractions from our schedule and run hard after Him alone. We do not pursue Jesus for His benefits that He gives, but we hunger just for Him.

Jesus is the Reward for Waiting

The Shulamite is pictured in bed when the bridegroom knocks at her door. It was not the appropriate time for fellowship; it was sleep time, so she hesitates. Finally, her emotions are stirred to see him, so she gets up and goes to the door to find that he is gone. Her heart sinks at his departure but she does not stop there. She runs through the city calling to him. The next time they are pictured together they are coming out of the wilderness and she is leaning on her beloved. *(Read Songs 5:2, 8:5)*. Jesus had stopped answering me through the noise I had created. He refused to respond to my self-imposed deadlines. Instead, Jesus would come at the most inopportune time. Have you ever multi-tasked God? I love to drive and pray at the same time. I still do it to this day. However, during this season of my journey, the Lord let me know that He was offended that I did not consider Him worthy of my undivided attention. Another course correction was placed in front of me as I learned the worth of rearranging my life and my guarded schedule for Him. As in the case of the Shulamite, the question remains for us. Will we follow Him into the wilderness in order to encounter Him on His terms? ✝

Personal Journal Entry
January 12, 2005

"And now also the axe is laid to the root of the trees: therefore every tree which brings not forth good fruit is hewn down, and is cast into the fire." Matt. 3:10

"For if the firstfruit is holy, the lump is also holy: and if the root be holy, so are the branches." Rom. 11:16

It seems that God is taking me and the elders at Victory back to examine everything that we do. We are to question why we started doing them and where they came from.

It is ironic how we spend our lives trying to minimize risk, trying to control our circumstances. God takes us to a place where our circumstances are anything but controlled. It seems His whole preliminary work in us is to disqualify us before we can be qualified.

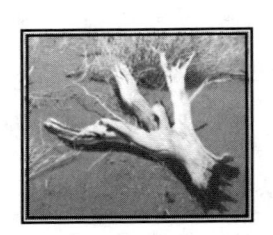

Chapter Five
DESPERATE LEADERS FOLLOW JESUS

"Then Jacob said, 'O God of my father Abraham and God of my father Isaac, the LORD who said to me, 'Return to your country and to your family, and I will deal well with you: I am not worthy of the least of all the mercies and of all the truth which You have shown Your servant; for I crossed over this Jordan with my staff, and now I have become two companies. Deliver me, I pray..." (Gen 32:9-11 NKJV).

Jacob had reason to fear as he faced his brother, but fear would not stop Jacob from his God-appointed meeting with Esau. Jacob quickly reminded the Lord of His promise and asked, once again, for His mercy as he walked to the meeting place. He knew that if it had not been for the mercy of God, the presence of God, and the promises of God, Jacob's life was sure to be over. He laid his destiny completely in the hands of his God and did not allow fear to stop the reunion with the brother whom he had betrayed. As we read this story of Jacob, we hear the stress that is on this man. He works to minimize his losses by dividing his family into two groups, but there is no guarantee how this is going to turn out. He is throwing himself on the mercy of God and the mercy of his brother, Esau. At what point does the risk outweigh the reward? Do you think that there may have been concerned family members who might have counseled him to cancel his appointment with his brother? To be sure, Rebekah most likely would have done so, if she had still been alive!

The Visitation of Jesus

There are many romantic ideas about the life and ministry of Jesus. As I was initially going through deepening sorrow over my own selfishness, I had not stopped long enough to consider that He might be responsible for offending my heart. However, there are many accounts of such things in the Bible. Jesus, Himself would offend a person or a crowd of people to find those who were desperate. To those who would pass the test, to not keep the offense in their hearts toward Him, He offered the reward of His presence. We may have some of those same romantic notions today. We desire the visitation of Jesus in our church, but we must understand that when He comes, He comes as He is, not as we want Him to be. That means that many of the things that Jesus will say and do will be offensive to our minds and understanding. As it turns out, we learned that Jesus is much more concerned about our spiritual welfare than what offends us. This example was also the case with a Canaanite woman who came to Jesus. *"Then Jesus went thence, and departed into the coasts of Tyre and Sidon. And, behold, a woman of Canaan came out of the same coasts, and cried unto him, saying, 'Have mercy on me, O Lord, thou Son of David; my daughter is grievously vexed with a devil.' But he answered her not a word. And his disciples came and besought him, saying, 'Send her away; for she crieth after us.' But he answered and said, 'I am not sent but unto the lost sheep of the house of Israel.' Then came she and worshipped him, saying, 'Lord, help me.' But he answered and said, 'It is not meet to take the children's bread, and to cast it to dogs.' And she said, 'Truth, Lord: yet the dogs eat of the crumbs which fall from their masters' table.' Then Jesus answered and said unto her, 'O woman, great is thy faith: be it unto thee even as thou wilt.' And her daughter was made whole from that very hour"* (Matt. 15:21-28 KJV).

Notice that at the cries of the woman, Jesus first ignored her. To make matters worse, the disciples, taking their cue from Jesus' non-response, thought that He did not want to be bothered with her, so they encouraged Him to send her away. Can you imagine how this woman felt as she cried and pleaded with the One whom she had seen heal and help so many others? She must have wondered what in the world was wrong with her! Why didn't she rate the same loving behavior Jesus had shown others who were bold enough to seek Him? What Jesus does next is simply alarming! He calls this woman of Canaan a dog. There is no softening these words to make them more acceptable. We even find it uncomfortable to read and teach this message, at times, because of what appears to be harshness from our Savior – our Groom – our own First Love.

He tells her that He is not called to take care of her issues. Most of us would have considered this the door slamming shut, and we would have walked away. Who could or would tolerate such a statement – such treatment? This Canaanite did not see this as the door slamming shut, but she saw the Savior cracking the door open to provide for her–*if* she could pass the test.

Desperate Leaders Follow Jesus

Leaders who do not pass this kind of test from the Lord, are leaders who are not desperate enough to come to the end of themselves and lose all pride for the sake of the calling. God is serious about those He has chosen. Many are called, but few are chosen, and you can be assured that He will test us in many ways to establish this. Our congregation at Victory Fellowship was the proverbial daughter in the story about the Canaanite woman. Victory Fellowship was also very sick. We were not seeing many signs that Jesus was pleased with us, but it did not seem to matter because we had now come to the place of being desperate. Jesus, in His mercy, had come to us and offended us by challenging our foundation. It was up to us to respond in faith, in the face of offense, and not to walk away with our pride. Were we willing to obey in order to have just the crumbs that Jesus dropped off His table? Were we willing to give up our sophisticated way of measuring success in our church and begin to use the measurement of Jesus and God's true approval of us? What is the use of having a church if God won't attend? We knew our pride would have to go in order to have God present with us.

How Does Jesus Spell Success?

At the height of Jesus' ministry, there was a very large crowd following Him. He had performed some remarkable miracles, and the news of His power and authority spread. At a point when I, if I had been doing the ministry of Jesus, would have been putting together strategy to take us to the next level, Jesus tested the level of the followers' dedication to the truth of His message.

He then preached the following sermon: *"Then Jesus said to them, 'Most assuredly, I say to you, unless you eat the flesh of the*

Son of Man and drink His blood, you have no life in you. Whoever eats My flesh and drinks My blood has eternal life, and I will raise him up at the last day. For My flesh is food indeed, and My blood is drink indeed. He who eats My flesh and drinks My blood abides in Me, and I in him. As the living Father sent Me, and I live because of the Father, so he who feeds on Me will live because of Me. This is the bread which came down from heaven--not as your fathers ate the manna, and are dead. He who eats this bread will live forever" (John 6:53-58 NKJV).

Jesus did not just preach this truth; He drove this point home by emphasizing it over and again. The result of Jesus' message that day was predictable, *"From that time many of His disciples went back and walked with Him no more"* (John 6:66 NKJV). Jesus did not preach His message to shrink the numbers of His followers, but it was and continues to be a message that offends and sifts those who are not truly surrendered.

According to Jesus, this message is essential to life and growth and the maturity of the kingdom of God. If we are measuring success by dollars and numbers, we might conclude that the risks for loss are too great if we teach such a truth. We might even reason that it would be irresponsible to preach in such a straightforward way. Our alternative is to water down the essential offensive messages to make them more palatable to our compromised ways. We will not walk past our comfort zones to put Isaac on the altar so that God can give him back. This equates to lack of faith, and without faith, it is impossible to please God.

The truth is that if we want the presence of Jesus, it is imperative that we follow Jesus' ways. It must be acceptable to have people (and their money) leave. In our case, we knew

God had called us to sincerely bless people as they chose to leave our church. We even were to be sure they were planted in a church where they were able to grow and have their needs met. It was not easy for us to make these transitions. We had worked diligently for many years to grow into what we had deemed successful. In the past, if a family left our church, we would make an effort to persuade them to stay. We had once considered ourselves a failure when people walked out the doors and did not return. God called us to this humble place of losing our congregation as we desperately sought His way of doing things. Those who were not comfortable with what God was doing in our midst, were invited to leave peacefully and with our blessing.

More Provoking from God

God also began to provoke us to examine why we did everything that we did. For example, why did we separate the family unit immediately upon their entering our church? We would send the different age groups to different departments as soon as they arrived through our doors for services. Why did we spend so little time in prayer? Why did we take attendance? I have a three-inch binder with growth studies for the past fifteen years along with tithing statistics. Why did we do this? It reeked of the place King David found himself when he took a census and was severely reprimanded by God's prophet. Just like King David, we were relying on numbers instead of on God. I would always reason that we needed this information to calculate whether the resources were available for the next new project. The Lord began to show us how many of these practices of our church were offensive to Him.

We repented to God, again, and stopped doing what was offending Him. As we look back over the course of the past several years, as we removed those things that displeased God, He was faithful to put it on our heart to implement the things that would please Him.

We began calling the congregation to an hour of prayer before each service. The teens began to meet for prayer before their weekly meetings. The elders began to pray together weekly for God to continue to lead them. We have also initiated fast days for all who can and will participate. As we continued doing this, it cemented our sincerity toward God and His ways. Our hospitality group started monthly fellowship lunches to connect people who were otherwise disconnecting from one another. Children started staying with parents during worship and are participating in communion together as a family, which we began commemorating each week. Later, we added prayer teams at the front altar during worship.

A short time later, the Lord led us to add prophecy teams available for anyone who needed to hear from the Lord. The Lord was coming to lead us, and He watched to see if we would trust Him and continue to follow. Once we laid down our own agendas and began to wait on Him to give instruction, God was faithful each time we took a step forward, to meet us with instruction.

Turning a Large Ship

We have touched a bit on this huge undertaking being like changing the direction of a large ship. One of the man-made arguments for not following Jesus may be that, *"it takes such a long time to turn this big ship around."* Perhaps the answer to this line of thought would be in asking ourselves, *"What kind of ship are we on?"*

In a time of war, if a ship is ordered to turn from a certain coordinate to go in a different direction, there is an understanding that lives are in danger. The person who is in charge of the vessel does not have the perspective that the Generals in charge do, nor does he have the luxury to question the orders.

The Commander of the Boat is obligated to do exactly as ordered as quickly as possible. We have to be honest and accountable for what our High Commander is speaking in these days. There is a need to help people understand the reason for turning the ship, and we know that it takes time to prepare for new mindsets. On the other hand, if we use this as an excuse in hopes of staying the course because of the risk of loss, I only need remind you of the Titanic.

The Captain of the Titanic, prideful of his unsinkable ship, ignored numerous warnings about the water conditions. I am sure that the guests on board the Titanic would have overlooked arriving late or experiencing some discomfort if it would have meant not drowning in the icy ocean.

Studies show that the church could use some directional change, heed the warnings and stop their present course. Researcher, George Barna reports in his book, <u>Revolution, Finding Vibrant Faith Beyond the Walls of the Sanctuary</u>, some startling findings:
> *"Eight out of ten believers do not feel they have entered into the presence of God, or experienced a connection with Him, during the worship service."* [1]

"The typical church believer will die without leading a single person to a lifesaving knowledge of and relationship with Jesus Christ." [2]

"Only 9 percent of all born-again adults have a biblical worldview" [3]

"Fewer than one out of every six churched believers have a relationship with another believer through which spiritual accountability is provided" [4]

This is only a sampling of many alarming facts that Barna's studies have found in the American church. It is sobering to read this and the additional information he provides.

Charting the New Course

Our early days of change were anything but smooth. We were transitioning from something that was very familiar onto an uncharted course, all of which we had very little if any understanding. We could have made our congregation feel much more confident about where we were going, if only we knew where God was leading us. That is what faith is all about. It is the evidence of what is not seen. We were called out of our comfort zone to believe God and trust Him. Those who stood with us through the transition, and saw what happened, found new faith with each new thing God brought to our fellowship.

The elders serving with me at that time were loyal participants in the new course that had been set for the church. Navigating was done with a team that prayed, fasted and had God-given input into where we were heading. We did not all share the same opinion at times, and it was at those times that we stopped and continued to seek the Lord until we all had the same directive. It was not always pretty, but it worked. Thankfully, on that early team, was a leader with a prophetic gifting, Rick French. What an invaluable gift he was and is to us. Another elder, Scott Maskell, sees things as they are and has a way of saying the obvious that everyone else has missed. Jim Nichols and his family have worked along side us for so long, I cannot remember when they were not with us. His passion for Jesus and commitment to God's voice is absolutely contagious. The new elders who have joined with us were like fresh recruits in the battle at the right time. God brought new wine to the new wineskin that He had created. Brent Gireoux, Vince Baker and Artez Young are all valued prayer warriors. They carry an anointing for prayer and praise that leads us into worship, God's way. There have been many times when answers would come from the lips of one of the elders in a season of praying, and we all would have an overwhelming sense of the direction from the prayers.

There is a sense of urgency in the hour in which we live, for leaders who will follow the call when it is heard. Thankfully, those who stayed with us as we made our way through the unknown were willing to be called up to a higher level. We received much needed encouragement from people to continue. We, as the leaders who survived and are thriving under God's new command, give our heartfelt and sincere appreciation to the body of believers who we have been so privileged to serve for over 20 years. There have also been many who have joined with us *during* our journey and many more have joined us *because* of our journey, to whom we also want to express our appreciation. These are the soldiers of

Desperate People in Desperate Times

this journey, who heard the call of Jesus coming from their leaders. It was not an eloquent or a well-rehearsed message that we presented to them, but it was as if the Lord was commanding His troops to the battle of their lives and for their lives.

The urgency of the message matched the intensity of God speaking through His prophet Joel. *"The LORD gives voice before His army... 'Now, therefore,' says the LORD, 'Turn to Me with all your heart, with fasting, with weeping, and with mourning.' So rend your heart, and not your garments; return to the LORD your God, For He is gracious and merciful, slow to anger, and of great kindness; and He relents from doing harm. Who knows if He will turn and relent, and leave a blessing behind Him – a grain offering and a drink offering for the LORD your God? Blow the trumpet in Zion, consecrate a fast, call a sacred assembly; gather the people, sanctify the congregation, assemble the elders, gather the children and nursing babes; let the bridegroom go out from his chamber, and the bride from her dressing room. Let the priests, who minister to the LORD, weep between the porch and the altar; let them say, 'Spare Your people, O LORD, and do not give Your heritage to reproach, that the nations should rule over them. Why should they say among the peoples, 'Where is their God?' Then the LORD will be zealous for His land, and pity His people. The LORD will answer and say to His people, 'Behold, I will send you grain and new wine and oil, and you will be satisfied by them; I will no longer make you a reproach among the nation"* (Joel 2:11-19 NKJV).

A New Evaluation

Joel's call was intended to wake the nation to realize their spiritual condition and call them to repent. It was a promise that God would pity His people, and He would bless His people with everything that they have need of so that they would become a blessing to the earth once again. God's strategy is not to assemble the greatest military minds at the table to evaluate our strength. Our strength is in our humility toward God and our willingness to follow Him at all costs. We call the fasts as we weep and mourn for *our* condition of compromise to be cut away from us. Our hearts need to be circumcised. We are to allow God to sanctify what we have defiled as we become willing to do the purpose of God and follow Jesus once again.

Finding Partners

Thankfully, we did not have to make this journey alone. Although there are not too many voices who are speaking in these terms, we found a few. The first we heard came from Rhonda Hughey and her team at Fusion Ministry. They provided encouragement and counsel along the way that helped sustain us. They coached us through many battles. When we made the decision to move in this new direction, my wife, Carolyn, was right by my side. She was in total agreement with every step and never once questioned anything. I do not believe that it would have been possible for us to move in this direction without the support that the Lord sent to us. Further, I would not recommend any leader radically change directions in their own ministry without the full support of their spouse. It was comforting and imperative that the Lord spoke to my wife in her own time of devotions and how the Lord brought her into agreement with me enabling us to proceed as one in Christ. I praise God, daily, for a loving and God fearing wife. There are those forerunners from other nations who had gone before us. We made every effort to listen and apply what we were hearing from them as well – always filtering and confirming any directive with God. What a pleasure it was to spend ten days with more than forty transformational leaders from over twenty-five countries at the Global Transformation Summit in Brazil. Very early on in my time with these other leaders, I became keenly aware that this would be a rare blessing for me and other leaders from America.

Brazil – June 2008 – A Nation in Transition

Brazil is a nation that is beginning to experience the manifest presence of Jesus in amazing ways. The Brazilian people are very loving, social people, so each leader was only too happy to give time for anyone to ask many questions. Leaves glow at night on some of the mountainsides where believers gather to hold all night prayer vigils. The leaders of the Brazillian churches also told the story about a city that had experienced years of drought whose citizens had turned to satanic spiritualists for help. For more than four years, a united city church went to a place on the side of a mountain to pray every day and many times all night. One day, while on the way to the place of prayer, they witnessed water flowing in the river bed that had been dry the day before. When they reached the place where they prayed, water was gushing from under a rock and has since provided water for the city. Many are turning to the Lord as a result of these miracles. Remember, the Word of God says that signs and miracles will follow us! We don't need to be busy trying to make these things happen. If we are in God's will and are seeking

Him and His presence, these things cannot help but manifest themselves! All of creation groans to see the Sons and Daughters of God revealed. In all of my interviews with these leaders, without exception, not one of them mentioned any of these miracles! I had to ask specific questions about these things. Their answers were absolutely surprising. While they gave glory to God for these things in nature, they were careful to say that these were not the most important or significant things that were happening but rather a result of the most important things that the church was doing. Pastors are repenting to one another for jealousy, a competitive spirit. Leaders are coming together on a regular basis for accountability and getting to the root issues in the city. This, I found refreshing!

I had the opportunity to visit several of the places where these believers pray night and day. One was on the second highest mountain top in the city of Belo Horizonte. The highest point is also a place where believers hold night and day prayer. These two points are about three to four miles apart from each other. On one of the days, a group of seven of us visitors arrived in our van, which had taken us part way up this mountain side. We parked and walked across the street to a broken up sidewalk to make our way to the entrance gate. As we walked on the sidewalk, a presence began to envelop all of us. It was a sweet presence of Jesus, there to greet us like a welcome mat for all who entered. We responded to His presence with tears and laughter. The Lord surely had our attention. Gone were the conversations about the lovely meal we had or any other small talk. We all entered through the gate and started up the two hundred foot incline. As we

Desperate People in Desperate Times

did, we began to hear the cries that were coming from the top of the mountain, men and women who were pleading with God for their city. This mountain top had become a place where the Lord leans close to hear His people and respond to their prayer.

As I moved close to these people who were crying out, I was overcome by the burden, their burden for the city, and could do nothing except weep and join the chorus of the desperate cries for the souls of Belo Horizonte. Every breath I breathed in was as if I was breathing in the burden and the presence of the Lord. Out of that burden, I began to cry out for the souls in a city whom I did not know, but it was with such genuine fervor – in a way I had never done in my own city. It was obvious that these people had counted the cost of following Jesus, decided to follow and now God, Himself, had come close to them and made certain places His habitation. Brothers and sisters in Christ, God is looking for a place to put His Name. Will you open your heart and community – your church – to Him? Will you lay it all down so that He can pick you up and help you do things His way?

Chapter Five Endnotes
1. George Barna, "Revolution" Tyndale House Publishers, Inc. 2005, 31
2. Ibid., 32
3. Ibid., 32
4. Ibid., 34

Personal Journal Entry
April 14, 2005

Oh that My people would harken unto Me...I should soon subdue their enemies, and turn My hand against their adversaries." Ps. 81:13

"I will go and return to My place, till thy acknowledge their offence, and seek My face." Hos. 5:15

Today I am learning that waiting is a value of the Kingdom of Heaven. Waiting is not something to be tolerated, i.e. if I have enough patience I will make it through this waiting that I have to do – attitude.

If I see waiting in this way I will be as Saul who was impetuous in his decision making.

I have been so impetuous in my life – Father help me to work the value of waiting on You into my core.

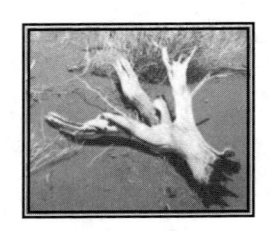

Chapter Six
A Generation of Desperate People

"Who may ascend into the hill of the LORD? Or who may stand in His holy place? He who has clean hands and a pure heart, Who has not lifted up his soul to an idol, Nor sworn deceitfully. He shall receive blessing from the LORD, And righteousness from the God of his salvation. This is Jacob, the generation of those who seek Him, Who seek Your face" (Ps. 24:3-6 NKJV).

Can you imagine a generation of Jacob-hearted people? That is what David, the Psalmist is envisioning, yes – even prophesying in the above verses. He is not speaking of just one person; Jacob, but a Jacob *generation* who have **"clean hands;"** which represents their lifestyles, and **"pure hearts;"** or a clean conscience before the Lord. There is much to do in the area of tearing down the idols that we have bowed our hearts before if we want the **"blessing from the Lord."** Whatever the cost, His manifest presence is absolutely worth the sacrifice.

As these verses indicate, the Lord's restored glory in the church and city is not because our agendas have captured the attention of heaven and resulted in the blessing of the Lord. Restored glory is the result of the abiding presence of Jesus in a community whose collective hands and hearts have been cleansed. It was true when King David wrote this, and it will be true in our day, when a compromised church cleanses their hands and purifies their hearts, the Lord promises His blessing.

The attraction of the church, before my generation, had never been its buildings, programs, or its sophisticated strategies! It was the manifest presence of the Lord. When He is present, He provides the magnetism that draws people to Him. There are many testimonies that attest to this in history. The late Arthur Wallis wrote about this in his classic book, <u>In The Day of Thy Power</u>;

"*As we survey the situation, we may well inquire with Gideon, "And where be all the wondrous works which our fathers told us of?" (Judg. 6:13) Is this all that God can do in the face of the appalling need on every hand? Are we forever shut up to the obvious limitations of modern evangelism? Must we never hope to see that mightier working that truly touches the masses at every level and compels them to face the implications of the gospel? Shall there never be a day of God's power, when our organization, and publicity, and inquiry room technique shall by superseded by the resistless power and faultless control of the Holy Spirit?*

Of course, God expects us to do our part in drawing souls under the sound of the gospel. It required no outpouring of the Spirit to bring Simon Peter to Jesus, it needed only the invitation of Andrew, his brother (John 1:41-42). But, where the normal means are failing to achieve the necessary end, it is of no avail to adopt the extra special means. If the natural means do not suc-

ceed we must look to the supernatural...We may be sure that when God begins to work, the people will be there, drawn not by invitation or persuasion, but by that divine magnetism that operates in revival." [1]

Before God showed Himself at Victory Fellowship, we had become so distracted by the sin that was present *in us* from all of our activity. We were busy doing good things, which had the effect of anesthesia toward our spiritual condition. The fact that the programs did not produce what was advertised only gave us tenacity to move on to the next most popular program out there.

We thought we were sincere in our hearts, but we were sincerely wrong and were drifting off into the wrong direction. Today, the seats at Victory Fellowship are now being filled with new occupants. There were many vacant seats for quite some time because of people finding other places to worship while we got ourselves in line with God's purpose for us.

These new worshippers are not all coming from other churches. We are finding that most who are making their way to our services are believers who had been disconnected and disillusioned with all the churches they attended. They could not find God! They were attracted to our church because of what they did not see. Gone were the days of hype and exaggeration. Gone were the days of a leader announcing that, *"the Lord is in this place."* When Jesus is with us, He does not need to be announced – He announces His own presence. It is not just a feeling, but a healing or a dramatic manifestation of His glory. God does not need our help to manifest Himself – once He is genuinely invited!

Some of the most dramatic manifestations of His presence have been during spontaneous times of repentance. This usually happened during times of praise and worship. No one announces, "*It is now time to repent of sin;*" it just happens. Someone may approach one of the elders to ask if they could have the opportunity to repent of an offense or a heart of unforgiveness. When they are released to publicly repent, the floodgates of heaven seem to open and the invitation to repent is opened by the Holy Spirit to all who feel the need to do so. In this atmosphere, it is difficult to stand upright as we sense that the pleasure of the Lord is with us, and all we can do is bow before Him. At other times, the church is filled with a wonderful time of celebration and praise.

For us, as the Body of Christ, we spent a long season going through a consecration process to purify our hearts and cleanse our hands. We received good counsel early in our journey that we should not expect a quick fix to our condition. Those of us in leadership were tempted, many times, to take back the reins again because things were not going as quickly and as smoothly as we would have liked. It seemed the troops were scattering at times, but we had to wait on God and let Him do things His way. We were well aware that these days would redefine our identity and set the path for, not only our future, but for the future of those God gave us to serve.

A Restored Identity

In the teaching of Jesus on the mount, He describes the lifestyle of those who will follow Him. There are three statements in Jesus' message that are marked with the words, *"when you...,"* meaning that these actions would be constant in the believer's life. They are: *"when you pray," "when you fast,"* and *"when you give to the poor."* See Matt. 6:2,5,16. The importance that Jesus places on these lifestyles became apparent to us, and for the first time in many of our lives, there was a genuine appetite for fasting, prayer and a complete giving of ourselves.

Our prayer time was energized with direction from heaven. Our church culture was directly affected by the internal consecration that was first wrought in the leaders then spread to the congregation. We were moving from what was an inward reality to a collective expression of the Body of Christ. The work of leading a group to "ascend the hill of the Lord" remains our primary focus today. It is the desire of the leadership of Victory Fellowship Church to sustain an atmosphere where it is normal for God's people to be completely transparent.

If we are to succeed in ascending the hill of the Lord and stand in His holy presence as a generation, the leadership's primary work was to translate what had happened in us as leaders to the body of believers. Our second focus remains to call back the entire church to the very fundamentals of the gospel. We interpreted the message of Jesus in His sermon on the mount as a call to those fundamentals.

Our message to our generation is a call to the place of prayer, fasting, and giving ourselves to the needs in our community. However, this is not a new identity, but it is our restoration to what Jesus called His people to walk in and through. Our new identity was that we were in this together – all the way – and we were and are becoming one with God and with each other. We have become identified with the true Body of Christ – the Bride of Christ whom God is preparing for His Son to come and gather unto Himself.

A Generation Who Prays

Victory Fellowship has not been alone in our quest for the presence of the Lord in the city. While we as a congregation were wrestling through our metamorphosis as a church, God was connecting like hearted pastors and leaders who began to pray together on a weekly basis. What was attracting the attention of heaven was a new unity among a small group of three, then four pastors who simply committed to prayer and fasting together. Then we began to bring our congregations together for evening services where we would all worship and pray together as an extended family.

We all knew that we must seek for the Lord's presence and that He was not always willing to respond to our first request. It is the *"honor of God to conceal a thing"* and it is our responsibility to *"seek it out."* See Prov. 25:2. The Lord sent us many challenges through a few different people who told us that we were moving in God's direction. The momentum really began to change when five congregations participated in a time of unified prayer and fasting for twenty-one days. This time of a collective consecration is called, <u>the Divine Experiment.</u>[2] Those involved focus on God's instruction to Solomon on restoring covenant relationships, a Biblical principle shown to us in 2 Chronicles 7:14. This fast was unique in that it emphasized a focus on separating ourselves from the culture and influence of the world. In order to do that, we put our church programs on pause, we cancelled unnecessary meetings, we turned our televisions off, we limited our time shopping and time spent on meaningless entertainment, etc. Hundreds of people committed themselves to seek God together in an intentional way for three weeks. We recognized that if we were going to prepare our congregations and communities for more of God's presence, we needed to start dealing with our own hearts before God. During this time, we focused our time on collectively praying every day, seeking God in humility, intimacy and repenting for any individual or collective sin He revealed to us. We repented to one another and to family members as God showed us things that needed to be addressed.

Each Sunday, the churches used the time normally spent preaching to share testimonies of what God was doing in the hearts of those involved in the Divine Experiment — in their hearts and in their homes. As a result of this, worship time became a place that overflows with great joy that reached out into homes and into the community. When we stepped out of our stubborn fleshly mindset and allowed the Holy Spirit to examine our hearts and lives, we found that we were broken, fragmented and weak people. Our pride, indifference and unbelief became easy to identify. All that we could do was to repent to God and to one another.

God responded to us in some amazing ways! Individuals were restored to intimacy with Jesus; hearts and bodies were healed. Family members were restored to healthy relationships. Families were reconnected when they replaced time spent watching television or engrossed in other forms of detached entertainment with time spent together praying, having meaningful dialogue and playing games as families. As our congregations humbled themselves and prayed together for those twenty one days, it strengthened our identity as a Body of Christ. This resulted in a new level of fellowship that we had never before experienced.

At the end of this experiment, the five congregations celebrated together by sharing testimonies and in thanking the Lord for how He met us. We knew we would never be the same! Our appetite for God's presence greatly increased. Our priorities changed. How we related to our families improved immensely. Our commitment to prepare ourselves to host the presence of the Lord in our hearts among our families, in the congregations and in the communities solidified.

J. Hudson Taylor wrote, "*The prayer power has never been tried to its full capacity. If we want to see mighty wonders of divine power and grace wrought in the place of weakness, failure and disappointment, let us answer God's standing challenge, 'Call unto me, and I will answer thee, and show thee great and mighty things which thou knowest not!'*"[3]

We unwittingly had stumbled into what Taylor wrote about. If we are to see a continuation of what has begun, both in our homes and in the church, it will be because we pray from our position of weakness and wait for God to operate from His place of strength. In a common quote seen and heard by W.S. Bowd, he said it this way, "*Prayer is weakness leaning on omnipotence.*" I was recently in two different cities in the United States. In each case, I was approached with a similar story about a prophecy that had been given regarding a revival that was coming to the nation through their city. "*Funny,*" I thought, "*the prophecy has also been given to our region.*" The conclusion that we must see is that God is about the business of bringing revival to the nation, and He will bring it through wherever the people of God commit themselves to focusing on His presence. What is it that brings His presence if it is not prayer? *"No learning can make up for the failure to pray. No earnestness, no diligence, no study, no gifts will supply its lack"* (E.M. Bounds).4

Proactive Fasting

Much of historical fasting has been reactionary. By this, I mean that a city or a nation is in a crisis, so the leaders call a fast. This happens in our personal walk as well. In the Old Testament, when God spoke to the people through the prophet, Joel, He gave a warning. The people had never seen anything like what was happening to their land as God judged them for their sin. What was the way to recovery? *"Now, therefore, says the LORD, 'Turn to Me with all your heart, With fasting, with weeping, and with mourning'"* (Joel 2:12). This is a fast called in response to the crisis, and it is always appropriate to respond to crisis in such a way. However, during the Babylonian captivity of Jerusalem, Daniel was reading the scroll of the prophet Jeremiah which foretold of the seventy year captivity of Jerusalem in Babylon:

"...I, Daniel, understood by the books the number of the years specified by the word of the LORD through Jeremiah the prophet, that He would accomplish seventy years in the desolations of Jerusalem. 3 Then I set my face toward the Lord God to make request by prayer and supplications, with fasting, sackcloth, and ashes. 4 And I prayed to the LORD my God, and made confession, and said, "O Lord, great and awesome God, who keeps His covenant and mercy with those who love Him, and with those who keep His commandments, 5 we have sinned and committed iniquity, we have done wickedly and rebelled, even by departing from Your precepts and Your judgments. 6 Neither have we heeded Your servants the prophets, who spoke in Your name to our kings and our princes, to our fathers and all the people of the land" (Dan. 9:2-6).

This was a wise and proactive move on Daniel's part. He was reminded of the prophecy as He meditated on God's Word, daily. Knowing that the time was near, what did he do? He did not sit and wait for it to happen. He entered into a time of repentance on behalf of his people, with prayer and fasting! As a result of Daniel's participation in fasting and prayer, he was not only involved in the fulfillment, but strategically used by God to bring about its fulfillment. Perhaps this is to be the new standard operating procedure of the church in America. So many prophecies have been given over our land, but who has entered into a place of faith by setting their face toward the Lord making supplications with fasting *until* we see His will fulfilled?

Brother Garcia was a young man of 18 years of age at the time of the Azusa Street Revival. He testified in the book, They Told Me Their Stories, that he had witnessed William Seymour's prophesy that in about 100 years there would be a return of the Shekinah Glory of God and that the revival to come would surpass the works of God at Azusa. The revival at Azusa Street ended around 1909, so we are living in the time of this prophesy's fulfillment.

Who will be the believers walking in faith who will set themselves in total obedience to see the fulfillment of this prophecy? This is but one of the many good words which the Lord God has given to His church. God is looking for partners who will come into such agreement with Him so that He can use us in the fulfillment thereof.

Finally, my primary purpose for writing this book is not to inspire. While inspiration is needed at times in the church, this is not one of them. What happened in my life when the

Desperate People in Desperate Times

leaders and I were encountered by Jesus was that we became a very broken and desperate people. It became impossible to "do church" in the same way as we had done it before. My desire and prayer for you is that, through this testimony, your heart would be broken and that your brokenness will lead you to desperation.

Our collective brokenness is much more precious and powerful to God than our creativity and ingenuity (Psalm 34:18). Desperate people, like Jacob, will leave the place of brokenness — stripped of pride, self-sufficiency and marked by God. The Jacob generation will awaken to divine destiny, which is the place where God gave Jacob, and will give us, His divine resources and restore His glory in His church. ✝

> Lord, God, we are desperate for You, and we need Jesus to lead us! Please send the sweet Holy Spirit to show us the way. Send Him into our hearts with conviction of Your truth so that we, too, may become a focused people – growing in number and strength – so that Your Word will spread throughout the land and all those for whom Jesus died, will be brought to You. God, please help our brothers and sisters to open their hearts and minds to find new direction so the ships that are heading in the wrong direction will be turned around and headed in Your direction. May we see ourselves in a mirror and come to repentance today! May we find You and need You in such a way that we cannot take our next breath until we know You are here. May we be so desperate for You. Let us be Your people, doing Your will in Your way and refrain from doing church our way. There are so many who have hearts that are toward You, and we pray a new beginning as You pour out Your Holy Spirit afresh upon Your people. AMEN.

Chapter Six Endnotes

1. Arthur Wallis, *In the Day of Thy Power*, Cityhill Publishing, 1988, 80
2. Rhonda Hughey, *The Divine Experiment* at *www.thedivineexperiment.com/devotions.php* by Fusion Ministries, Inc. 2004
3. Dr. & Mrs. Howard Taylor, Hudson Taylor's Spiritual Secret, *www.newchurches.com/mediafiles/hudson.pdf*
4. Edward M. Bounds, Power through Prayer, Scanned by Harry Plantinga, 1996. E-text is in the public domain. *www.leaderu.com/cyber/books/bounds/power.html*